A
BOOMER'S
VIEWS ON
LIFE, LOVE, GOD, AND FAMILY

WILLIAM LYNN SMITH

Order this book online at www.trafford.com
or email orders@trafford.com

Most Trafford titles are also available at major online book retailers.

Author Credits: Mary Agnes Smith

Printed in the United States of America.

ISBN: 978-1-4669-9245-0 (sc)
ISBN: 978-1-4669-9246-7 (e)

Trafford rev. 04/22/2013

 www.trafford.com

North America & international
toll-free: 1 888 232 4444 (USA & Canada)
phone: 250 383 6864 ♦ fax: 812 355 4082

Table of Contents

A Little Child Hides by William Lynn Smith

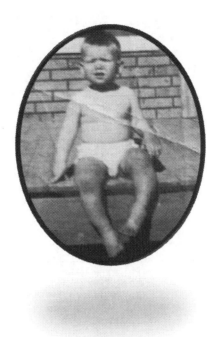

Inside every big ol' man on the face of the planet
A little boy resides to keep his flame alive and fan it.
Oh, he may not admit to the toddler's existence
But he's still there no matter how hard the resistance.
The little boy can be happy and the man will come out to play,
Or he can be mad and cause the man to pout pretty much all day.

What can we do with this knowledge we have acquired,
Now that we know that all men are this way wired?
How about the fairer sex; there is a fact not many knew:
Inside every grown-up woman is a little girl hiding too.

There are times she is petulant; times she is sweet.
She may want to play dress up or kick-the-can in the street.

These children hiding in us may embarrass us when they act.
They are probably less sociable and more matter-of-fact.
They don't understand and are hurt when not treated right.
It's hard for them to realize that when confronted they mustn't fight.
They are innocent and want to believe with all their hearts.
They don't have social graces; but they have street smarts.

Why do we harbor these children that refuse to grow up?
The ones that pick the most inopportune times to show up.
I'll tell you what I think, if you'll give me the time to explain,
It's not that they are our conscience; I think that fact is plain,
Because some of the little guys tend to stretch the truth a bit.
Some of them have trouble with a temper; I'm sure of it.
I believe they aren't hiding, I am pretty sure they must wait.
Waiting for that time when they will aid us at heaven's gate.

You see, Jesus told us that in life on this fact we must center
"Unless you become a little child, heaven you cannot enter"

So this is what this old railroader is going to do with the rest of his time.
I'm using all my parenting skills to make sure my little guy is just fine.
I'm going to just let him be a kid; never spoiling or making him frown,
Because he's going to be me in heaven after I lay my old body down.

A Servant's Heart by William Lynn Smith

She sits quietly because that is the only position that doesn't hurt;
Her back and hips have long since been worn down from all her work;
Too many loads of laundry, too many days standing over the sink,
Too many babies, too much of everything in life, I'm beginning to think.
She is a lovely person hiding inside a crusty business-like woman.
She is works hard and helps often; you can't say she's a showman.
She is attentive to anyone needing help; even at two in the morning.
But don't think she's easy; she can reduce you to ashes without warning!
How can you best describe someone like this? A really good start
Is that underneath her battle scarred armor beats a servant's heart.

So what do we do with an awesome warrior that has past her prime?
How can we show her that we appreciate the way she gave her time?
Repayment for her work or doing favors in return, is not what she expects.
She just wants her efforts to mean something that you can really respect.
But please don't make the mistake to believe her ego you can stroke,
That is to say; don't even think about using mirrors and blowing smoke.
She will see through that tawdry little charade right from the start!
And you really know that is not the way to treat her servant's heart.

I know that God has respected all her wishes and all her hard works.
I know that He is saddened about her body's aches and how it hurts.
So much so that he took our sadness and combined it to cover
The hurts and pains she has from her life time of service to others.
The devil thought he had the last laugh when Nancy and G passed.
What he made to be a monument to the chaos in our lives amassed,
Turned out to be our reward from the Master's planning table.
This is the truth that is told and not some little fable.

Air Castles by William Lynn Smith

Air Castles are a place I can go when I am where I don't want to be;
They're a special place I can retreat to and escape someone else's reality.
They are kind of like a vision, you know, a dream while you're awake
I take bricks of reality and use the mortar of imagination to make.
It started when I was a child on the farm "back in the day"
There were no elaborate toys for me to have with which to play.
My toys were blocks of scrap wood, clothes pins and string
With those items and my imagination I could have anything.
I had bulldozers to build roads in the cool dirt under the house.
Two by four tanks and clothespin infantry; the enemy to trounce.
God had provided me with all that a little feller needed:
Even my good dog Nipper to keep me safe and heeded.

It wasn't that my mom and dad were mean and not giving;
They were share croppers just trying to scratch out a living.
I wore clean clothes and had a warm dry bed to sleep in at night.
I can't ever remember seeing or hearing mom and dad fight.
We had loving family, good friends and always enough to eat;
Mom even managed to keep decent shoes on my fast growing feet.
Life was good and I found that I could play by myself for hours
Building towns and railroads in mom's beds of flowers

As I grew to adolescence from a cotton topped kid,
My imagination could get me into trouble and usually did.
It became clear that my air castles were a very private place to be.
I learned, by some hard life lessons, to keep that knowledge to me.
It seemed that I really wanted to share the visions of my youth;
The only trouble I encountered was I was telling them for the truth.
This practice is really frowned on by the folks living around you;
It can get a feller branded a liar and make folks quit listening too.
I am not a genius like my brother and it took me a while to get it.
You can't make up tales where you take reality, mold it and fit it.

I am sure some psycho babble clown could explain my behavior

The truth is I had not really learned the message from my Savior.

When Jesus took his disciples said "the truth shall set you free"

I now know beyond a shadow of a doubt, he was talking to me.

So I have taken this knowledge as a gift and refined it to be instructive.

Using my air castles to help me create rather than be destructive.

I have been known to attend mind numbing meetings that are real blowers

And spend that waste of time envisioning enhancements for lawn mowers.

You see my air castles don't take up all my cognitive space;

I usually use the reality around me to enhance and set the pace.

Like driving long distances and keeping myself alert;

I imagine that I am inspecting land to buy; to evaluate the dirt.

At times I can imagine what I would do if I had enough money.

Like buying all my friends whatever they wanted; pulling tricks; being funny.

Sometimes in reality Mary and I buy meals for people on the sly.

It is fun to watch them look around, wondering who and why.

Especially when the server tells them that an angel paid for their meals.

I have been blessed in my life and I want to show others how that feels.

Someday I would like to do more than buy a meal or give to charity.

But I am content, like Paul said, with my station in life and my giving ability.

So I will continue to stretch my mind around situations imagined,

Getting new ideas and refining those that I have already fashioned

Altitude of Your Attitude

by William Lynn Smith

Where is your attitude going today?

How do you react to what others say?

If someone treats you badly or just ignores;

Or you're in a meeting with a bunch of bores

Do you really want to wish them well,

Or secretly want them to burn in hell?

It is no secret; I am sure that it is true,

Your attitude looks just like you.

Yep. That's right; if your attitude is low

Like a whale in the deep with an anvil in tow.

Nothing said will help your downward trek

Until your life hits the ditch like a big ol' train wreck.

Others will gravitate away from the carnage

Only the closest ones will even offer a bandage.

You can usually see people like this along the way,

They usually treat you badly; that makes you stay away.

They continually drag their low attitude along the ground.

A fact that is signified by their perpetual frown.

It seems that they are lonely; I know that must be true.

Because they do their best to make others feel bad too

Just like always, God had a much better plan for us.

He knew that if we are happy with others and don't fuss

You know, that whole "love one another" thing

Will keep our attitudes up like birds on the wing.

If your attitude is high, soaring like an eagle,

It shows on your bearing, you look positively regal!

With a smile or even a laugh and a good word,

You can face any situation no matter how blurred.

But remember, a lot of evil hides in the shadows of our humor.

Jokes with sarcastic remarks can hurt, and that's no rumor.

Living with a good attitude and a smile on your face,

Is what God had in mind when He gave you His grace!

Angels by William Lynn Smith

Have you ever seen an angel? I mean really.

With wings of feathers and a robe that's frilly?

A half naked fat kid with curly blonde hair

And chubby red cheeks, flying through the air?

I know I haven't; at least not on this side of heaven.

And I don't believe all angels look like they're seven.

Nope, in the world as it is according to all the sages,

An angel can have many different faces and even ages.

I know one angel that lives in Memphis Tennessee,

The daughter of a man that is a best friend to me.

Michelle is a beautiful young lady with an angelic face.

She is smart and energetic, I could hardly keep pace.

All that is wonderful but it is not her angelic description,

She has no secret identity, no pass-word or encryption.

Michelle is an angel because she shows God's love,
She is proof positive that all love comes from above.
Her parents aren't lucky; they are extremely blessed
To be entrusted with an angel; as you might have guessed.

Another angel close to me is my grandson, Ryan.
This guy can make you feel good without really tryin'
He works hard and has a no nonsense approach to life.
His blessings are a beautiful daughter and Kia his wife.
Even though he has been dealt some tough cards for a player,
He knows that he will get through it with the power of prayer.
Now, his daughter Ellie could be an angel; She looks the part.
She is in training, and with Ryan and Kia she has a good start.

Let this be life lesson number whatever and one,
God is the master of all the universe, not just under our sun.
The word "angel" means minister and that's just what they do.
They are God's hands that he sends to minister to you.
Whether they are in a beautiful dress all clean and white,
Or in greasy coveralls that look like they lost the fight.
Keep your eyes and heart open good and wide.
Who knows, maybe you have an angel hiding inside.

Being a Christian (even when it hurts) *By William Lynn Smith*

I was on a business trip waiting for a plane

A gentleman was watching me with a look of distain

I fidgeted uncomfortably under his withering gaze.

Was I sitting in a personal hygiene failure haze?

Finally I deduced that he was looking at my lapel pin

A cross that my sweet wife of 40 years had given.

I struck up a conversation by saying "Is there something I can help you find"

He looked in my face, frowned and said "I think that is a symbol of a weak mind"

Taken aback and not really believing I had heard him right,

I decided to ignore the comment. "Are you on this flight?"

He continued his caustic track "What kind of God do you believe in?"

"All you do run around blaming the rest of us for acts of sin"

"You sit there all holier than thou with folded hands,

While children are starving and wars ravage the lands."

"What kind of God would let this bad stuff happen all around?

What kind of God would let wealthy industrialist spoil our ground?"

Well, here is where the training by my good Christian Mother came into play

It was plain as a diamond in a goat's navel I had three choices that day.

I could apologize for my entire "mindless Christian friend's" plight,

Or I could quietly unpin the cross, take it off and put it out of his sight.

Or I could take my tie off and wrap it around his scrawny neck

Then make this waiting area look like a really bad train wreck!

But I decided to take my Savior's instructions to heart

And see what I could do to help heal this poor man's heart.

"So you're a Democrat, I see. A liberal one at that"

I said in a business–like manner as in the seat beside him I sat.

"I voted Republican in the last election. The losing side of the room"

"It appears that we are on the road to ruin, four more years of gloom"

"It's beyond me how those idiots can call themselves leaders"

"All they know how to do is promise everything to heart bleeders"

The man's face became flush and his manner animated
It became clear that my comments made him quite agitated.
I knew there was no advantage to continuing this line of conversation.
But I just couldn't help a little "human" response to his vile oration.
I decided to show this man that there is a reality called Christian love
So I quickly spoke in a low and even tone before he started to shove.

I said "OK, now that we have all that mutual crap out of the way,
Let's start over and make this flight a little more enjoyable today."
"My name is William and I work for the railroad"
He said he was Frank and he was on his way to Crossroad.
We spoke about the beauty of Colorado and his wonderful horses.
He said he worked for an agency that handled emergency resources.
Through our conversation his demeanor seemed to soften
There was still an undercurrent of anger that happens so often.

At last he asked "Do you really believe in your God? To you it's not a fairy tale?"
"When you pray to Him are you still in love with Him even when He fails?"
He continued almost as if I wasn't there. "I don't know how to pray".
"Even if I knew exactly how to do it right, I wouldn't know what to say."
"In my job I help people that have lost everything they own,
Most of them crash and burn, many have melt-downs full blown"
He continued almost wistfully "Then there are the ones that we call mindless,
You know the ones. They don't seem to care about their plight, like blindness".
"My co-workers and I dismiss them as part of the house owning homeless throng
Now that the house is gone they are where they should have been all along."
He said "Most of them let everything go saying that God will provide.
They sit on their hands waiting for a handout. They have no pride."

I sat for some time quietly breathing a prayer to God for His wisdom.
I knew this man had a lifetime of anger and he needed God's freedom
"God is a lot of things to a lot of folks but He doesn't need defense
He has a plan for each of our lives. Only the ignorant take offense."
"Yes, I pray to Him in faith because I know He always hears.
It is that faith that gives me comfort and erases all my fears."

"Like a loving Dad, His answers don't always pass my understanding test.
But I have the faith that no matter what, His way is always the best."
I looked at him and said "Frank, in all this falderal it helps if you knew
That no matter what happens in your life the faith you have is up to you"
"You must know that God is the Creator of all that we are;
Everything from the smallest microbe to the largest star.

In my hands was a magazine with a picture of a building under construction
The picture showed guys working with tools and material following instruction.
I said "It is like this. All these guys don't see or understand the architects plan.
Yet they work hard at their tasks, their labor directed toward that plan.
That is the way we must be in this life. We all have a part in His overall plan.
Some of the parts may not make sense to us at the time but we should know
That it is His world and His plan that is for the good of all, not just for show.

Tray tables up and seat belts fastened the intercom urgently boomed.
The cabins' occupants began to prepare to leave our metal cocoon.
I don't know if I helped him but I did what I was directed.
I have faith that it was in God's plan, if not it will be corrected.
The last time I saw Frank we exchanged business cards in the gate.
I said "gotta go. It's cold outside and I hate to make Nancy wait"
"I'll continue to pray for you and yours Frank. I have faith that some day
Your heart will turn to God, you will find your faith and you will learn to pray."

As I walked away one last comment I couldn't help but Fling
"Once we clear that faith issue, let's work on that Democrat thing"

Bill the Burro by William Lynn Smith

Bill the burro lives up the street;
As donkeys go he's kind of neat.
He has a job at Hector's place.
He is a coyote guard; a top notch ace.
Ol' Bill is quiet, just stands around
Looking at nothing; just starin' at the ground.
As he runs, he just lopes along
He doesn't appear to be particularly strong.
But you let an interloper step on his grass,
And good ol' Bill will kick their . . . !!

Bridges by William Lynn Smith

The use of bridges is a very important part
Of the overland railway transportation art.
Because moving freight and folks from here to there,
Means bridges must be built and maintained with care.
The bridge must also instill confidence from the users,
That they won't end up in the ditch with bumps and bruises.

First, a bridge must have solid foundations;
Abutments and piers in good and firm relations.
No matter how impressive the upper works are,
Without good ground work, it won't even hold a car.
Second, the trestle works must be straight and sure.
A bridge is useless if it is so crooked traffic can't endure.
Third, the deck must be level and complete
The rail must have good ties on a solid seat.
Last, but most important of all, are the upper works:
Solid, but flexible, to roll with all the weight and jerks.
If the upper works were rigid and unable to give,
This big ol' bridge would have very long to live.
The bottom line of this list is the Maintenance of Way guys.
They must maintain the bridges daily regardless of the skies.
Because no matter how solid the construction,
Sloppy maintenance will cause its destruction.

In our lives and relations the bridges we build are important too.
If you don't think so, see what living totally alone does for you.
We reach out from the abutments of our life's borders
To establish communication and friendships with others.
Although that establishment is important as you may guess.
The maintenance of those bridges is also; a fact I must stress.

Exaggerations, half truths, overstatements and even lies
are terrible foundations for a bridge, no matter what its size.
If you think building a bridge is difficult to keep it from tumbling,
Try repairing one that was established on lie and is now crumbling.

The main truth about a bridge is "less is more".
The fewer the parts, the safer it will get us o'er.
So the bridge Jesus built to reach me is a beauty to behold.
He only used two rough hewn timbers and three nails to hold.
The maintenance of this bridge is important as well.
Although it is simple, it's sometimes very hard, I must tell.
Because to keep this bridge so my soul He can retrieve;
The one thing I <u>must</u> do is <u>in Him I must believe</u>.

Building Blocks by William Lynn Smith

When I was small, barely there at all, my mother used to tell me;
"Doctor Webb said you'd be big, not like a pig, but an oak tree, strong and tall".
"And it must be true" she moaned "cause you were born already half grown".
Those were the first blocks, the foundations of my life, placed there by love not strife.

During my first years, there were very few tears. After all I was the baby.
Wanda and Jess always said yes 'cause after all the I was the baby.
The blocks were stacked tall and straight, some say skinny as a rail.
My dad said with a chuckle "All this monkey needs is a tail"
My mother added blocks of love and sensitivity for all things weak or small,
My brother added a block of common sense, "do it right or not all";
My sister's block was independence, to balance with reliance;
"You ain't the boss of me", was her statement of defiance;
My dad's blocks were ones of pure gold. He placed them around my heart.
They were blocks of honesty and courage and that was only the start.
His example placed the block of Jesus providing the light I will need.
He showed me the Bible, the Word of God that I should heed.
He placed the block of a father's love, a pattern for me to copy.
The same block was in Jesse's life to help me when life got choppy.
The mortar that held these blocks so tight and so straight
Was the love of a family a much stronger bond than hate.

As my life passed by, many more blocks were added.
The sharp corners became worn and smooth but were rarely padded.
Life's bumps and bruises left their marks on the blocks;
But my family's love, support and humor kept me off the rocks.
Nancy lay the blocks of a husband's love and commitment.
She also placed the blocks of fatherhood on my stack.
We both learned how to live well, even when there was lack.
Jyll and Jessica lay the blocks of being a "daddy".
They made it easy to be a hero and not a "baddy"

Man, what a ride! But it is now the twilight of my years.

The cap stones are being placed by the falling of my tears.

The girls are making their own lives from the blocks we gave them.

They are doing well although I miss their misbehavin'

Nancy went on to be with Jesus. Gee, these blocks were hard to place,

I said "I'll be there soon and again I'll kiss your face".

But I am glad that the completion of my building was not in God's plan.

Apparently he had other ideas involving a gal who needed a good man.

Mary was alone since Gordy laid down to rest. She said "Ok, I've given it my best".

But Miss Pam put me in her way even though I did not want to join her group.

She said "you'd better get help from us or your life will turn into poop"

In the grief group I met Mary and she fit my life like a comfortable glove.

Although we both thought it impossible it appeared that we were falling in love.

Mary lay the blocks of acceptance and rebuilding lives thought to be on the rocks.

She provided four girls and a gaggle of grandkids that needed a place to put their blocks.

I am providing a father's love to one and all; teaching and reaching, leaving no one to fall.

They make it easy to be "Pop" or Grandpa Will; A roll in their lives I am happy to fill.

Sooner or later the cap stones will be placed. The building of my life will be complete.

All that remains is an inspection and then in heaven I will take my seat.

God is the inspector and of course even though the structure is not perfect.

Jesus will be there to answer all of the questions that God will have for the architect.

Country Folks by William Lynn Smith

Can we stop making fun of just plain ol' country folk?
I mean; is it a contest to see how much fun we can poke?
Did'ya ever wonder where the term "red neck" comes from?
How in the world did it ever become synonymous with dumb?
A feller's neck gets burned in the sun from working all day
Usually helping out on the family farm; without any pay.
Sure they have much simpler needs in life than most.
Sometimes a .22 rifle shooting a soup can off a post.
That can keep them entertained a whole afternoon.
It beats going to a mall and hanging out with some goon.
Country kids keep themselves amused by midnight cow tippin'
Some of the older ones sit behind the shed, sour mash sippin'
City kids get high on smoking a weed called marijuana.
I guess country kids could smoke it too if they wanna.
But that practice has been proven to cause them real harm.
Because using that stuff will land your butt in the penal farm.

Country kids get a really cool rush sliding down a grassy slope,
On an appliance cardboard box, less steering more hope!
City kids want to be recognized for cutting the lawn (how sweet)
Country kids operate a 12 ton combine to harvest the wheat.
Country kids live life to the full; work hard and play harder still.
They value life and, except for protecting and hunting, rarely kill.

Well, I guess I understand now and you know it is really sad.
City kids don't have a lot going for them; most of that is bad.
If it makes their lives just a little bit better to believe
That country kids are dumb as a stump, it may relieve
Them of the stigma that plagues those urban dwellers.
To find out that they are just jealous fellers

Define "Bad Things"

by William Lynn Smith

I have heard it asked "why do bad things happen to good folks?"

I don't know; it's kind of like "why do some eggs have two yolks?"

Things are always going to happen; that God's design and it is pretty sound.

Gravity holds us, water gets us wet and the wind can blow us around.

So what is a bad thing? Is it something that is evil or just odd?

Is a hurricane or earthquake some kind of punishment from God?

I don't think so, not really. You see God is more interested in how we are,

Not in our stuff; not our towns or cities, not our clothes or even the car.

When He was with us on the earth as Jesus; the Bible tells us clear,

That He told all his followers to love one another, hold their beings dear.

He didn't say that we should make sure to take care of our farms,

He didn't tell us to take care of the clothing that we have in our arms.

In fact the only thing he said about the stuff that we own was

not to be jealous and covet the things that your neighbor has.

OK, so what would Jesus define a "bad thing" as being

We know that He couldn't care less about our things

I think He says that it is not the wind or rain that causes us loss,

It is the way we react to them and the damage they cause.

The damage is done to our spirit by the fear and the anger

We feel from bad weather or a death of someone that we hold dear.

No, the bad thing doesn't need to be a horrible occurrence causing us to run.

It can simply be an insidious disease quietly stealing the life of a loved one.

It is what we do, how we act, that makes the times good or bad.

If we don't "love one another" like we have been taught, it makes God sad.

That love is the example of how neighbor reaches out to help neighbor,

After the storm passes, that love and help replaces all the fear and anger.

Death was defeated by Jesus when he sacrificed Himself on the cross.

That means when our loved ones leave us, we shouldn't count it as a loss.

When the death of a loved one is totally unexpected

It may be so hard for you that you thoughts can't be collected.

Just know that God is in control and is never surprised.

What you see as a sad loss, is really your loved one's prize.

We must know that death is only the doorway to another life

We must go through it to leave this world of pain, sadness and strife.

I am sure that we will be eased if we know at the end,

Jesus will meet us at the gate saying "Well done; Welcome friend".

Flight of the Dodo by Mary Agnes Smith

It started with a passing, a long illness finally over,

He left them all with empty hearts, one maybe more than others.

No one could guess the pain they felt that cold day in November.

Least of all the oldest son, so many memories to remember.

Then he began to see his life as wasted time and trials.

Just moving here and flying there a lot of empty miles.

He had those kids, all grown up now and making their own lives.

They wouldn't really need him now but, what about his wife?

Oh, he believed she would understand and he would have the time he wishes,

To "see what's out there" you know, look around. That didn't see so selfish.

He really just wants that "freedom", for him that is no doubt.

He'll "find himself" in just a bit and then he'll work it out.

That's quite true I guess but then, at whose expense.

That is the part he doesn't know, his thoughts are on the fence.

She's beautiful, his wife, that is true. But has those few small flaws.

And he deserves the BEST you know. The kingdom, queen and all.

A local yokel, no he's not, no country bumpkin guy.

He's smart and hansom; a Navy captain and beside that he can fly.

He has it all no one doubts; he's really quite a catch.

Unfortunately not smart enough to know he has the perfect match.

A wife like his, they're hard to find. She'll wait a little while.

Let's hope the boy becomes a man and stops acting like a child.

The cost of "freedom" is often greater than the price he will pay.

And I believe, as does his wife, he will find that out someday.

That life that he is looking for is an illusion and he has no other plan.

When he finally "finds himself" he'll find a very lonely man

Frisco 104 by William Lynn Smith

I had to drive by the railroad yard some task to complete

My route took me by the white lead track just off the street.

Old locomotives, worn out and have been pushed out back,

No longer needed in service, just stored in the white lead track.

There is one that caught my attention, I stopped to see.

It is old Frisco 104, a switch engine, an Alco, I believe.

She stands serenely as if reflecting on her past,

She used to be quite strong but never very fast.

Once the pride of Memphis, black, gold and dapper;

She is now a rusting hulk; ready for the scrapper.

As switch engines go, she was about the middle of the pack;

She had plenty of punch when the hogger slammed 'er back.

The brass controls on stand were always gleaming.

The hogger's coffee cup sat there always steaming.

It's not very hard to sense the ghosts of the past

It seems that I can even hear her mournful horn blast.

I see lantern ring tail kick signals flashing like mini comets

Window shade canvases straining against their grommets,

One of Detroit's finest diesels belching fire and smoke

Shoving and pulling cars of merchandise, coal and coke.

Sand dust billowing and an occasional hiss of the brakes

The work was hard but this old engine has what it takes.

The foreman holds his lantern by the bale; spinning it as if driven.

Bringing it down in an arc; another ring tail kick signal is given.

The hogger knocks the brakes off and slams the throttle to number 8

104's thousand horses leap; leaving the poor pin puller to his fate

From a standing start you almost see the pin puller flagging.

Two car lengths to kick speed; by that time he's almost dragging.

A "wash out" flag down is given by the foreman finally satisfied.

Another car load rumbles down the lead into a track; classified.

104's diesel trails off and brakes scream; almost disappointed
That it couldn't keep on until the pin pullers arms become disjointed.

We are both alike in many ways; old 104 and me.
We are both old now and the times have changed, you see.
I used to be that pin puller; although a lot lighter and faster then.
"Ten foot tall and bullet proof" a country boy with attitude blend.
Now 104's diesel has been silent for all these many years.
The crater grease has hardened around her traction gears.
I have spent too many days bound behind a manager's desk
My hair line is shrinking, my middle's spreading, and my stamina is less
104's paint has faded and no longer gleams like gold;
Her leather seats are crumbling away to dust and mold.
Like her my time on the line has come and gone.
Like me she has been retired and now she sits alone.
If machines have memories I am sure she has quite a few
I know mine can fill a boxcar or maybe even two.

Now I know that even in this somewhat sad time there is hope.
Even though Ol' 104 will not continue as she is, I can cope.
Sure they will scrap her and the metal will be melted down,
But it will be remade into another locomotive for this town.
Old 104's excitement and drive will still exist because I have to say,
It is in the young railroaders hearts that continue to come this way.

As for me; I know that recycling is not in my future
We know that is neither in God's plan nor His nature.
When my time comes I will simply go to a better place
And spend eternity looking at my saviors face.

Green Eyes By William Lynn Smith

When someone crosses our path in life
Whether for a long time or very short
We tend to use a physical attribute of theirs
To place them in a life file of sort
I met my Mary when my heart was hurt and raw
My beautiful Nancy had passed into death's maw.
She had fought her battle well, no quitter she
And Jesus rewarded her with bliss for eternity.
But I was left standing there after the gala departure done,
Everything in my life was divided by half, I was hurting and alone.

Friends and family held me back from the brink of insanity
Prodding and herding me to life's right path incessantly.
'Til at last a "grief group" meeting I was forced to attend
With a bunch of other poor souls their sanity to defend.
Miss Pam and Miss Kim moderated this crew of injured souls
To reintroduce us to life without our loving partners.
We were told that our "new normal" included our new rolls
In a world that had been torn apart by cruel circumstances
But then I saw Mary across the room it was awkward like in teenage dances.
She was there for her daughter J.J. that lost her only dad
Mary had taken care of him in good times and in bad

Now all that is left is to heal and know life must proceed.

I listened to their stories with attention both long and short

Every now and again, I would have a comment or retort.

Mary began to notice me out of the crowd in the meeting

Her attention was welcome, it didn't matter how fleeting.

Her smile was beautiful like bright white sea gulls in blue skies

But nothing, nowhere compared to her flashing green eyes.

Those eyes welcomed me into the life of a wonderful lady

Being around her was comfortable and honest, not a bit shady.

Over the next few months we became the closest of friends,

We laughed and played like kids and held each other when we cried.

My life began to mean something again, the devil must have lied.

He tried convincing me that it was over for us.

Our kids were trying to make our "twilight years" much less fuss.

But it looks like our God had another plan in mind

It seemed that many people needed this "old" couple to help them find

The way and the truth that their very existence exemplifies.

The way is Jesus and the truth is that God will help anyone if he only tries.

Happiness by William Lynn Smith

Happiness can be as plentiful as the air you breathe.

It can also be as elusive as a butterfly on the breeze.

Some people believe happiness hides in fortune and fame;

Some feel that happiness is won like a prize in a game.

My friend, you must realize that true happiness is God driven.

It's up to you to believe and receive it when it is given.

Heros by William Lynn Smith

Who are the heros in your life? What did they do to make them special?

Did they step in to stop the strife? Were they larger then others there?

I have found that a hero doesn't have to wear a badge or carry a gun.

Drive a fire truck or even be able to lift a ton.

A real hero is the guy that routinely puts the needs of others first you see

You know the kind, people that continually go that extra mile for others.

They can be folks in the bank or grocery store and mostly all the mothers.

Those are the heros in my world. It is over their heads our flag is unfurled.

Folks from Hoboken to Frisco that get up every day to provide for us

From throwing our papers, cooking our meals and even driving the bus.

Without these heros life would grind to a stop right now.

Can you imagine finding something to eat if the farmer didn't plow?

How about the garbage we generate and gather to dispose.

Without the regular garbage collections where would we be, do you suppose.

Next time you see a poster showing a brave policeman, soldier or firefighter.

Extolling them as the true American heros, please look a littler higher.

Look at the person hanging the poster and think of them if you please.

Making a living, paying bills, raising a family, you know that ain't a breeze.

So take the time and effort and go a little out of your way

To tell them "thank you" and do it in a very sincere way

Be kind and patient when things just don't pan out

Put other folks feelings first, don't act like a spoiled boorish lout.

Jesus said "love others as you love yourself" that wisdom is incomparable.

Can you imagine a world where we all take care of each other.

I think that what God intended for man to do was to keep his brother.

I'm Not Afraid by William Lynn Smith

I fear no man nor beast on earth, my God is with me.

His promise is of incalculable worth; it has set me free.

He's the One that made me six foot two and 340 pounds.

He's the One that gave me the ability to go a few rounds.

He's the One that provided me with peace no matter the odds.

He's the One that showed me the futility of all the other gods.

It was His conversation with the Arch Angel, the psalmist recorded,

That Freed me from fear and doubt no matter how sordid.

Fear, death, hell and the grave were defeated on Calvary,

Fulfilling the promise God gave Abram under the tree.

I am Adam's seed, my soul is bought with Jesus' blood.

So I have no fear when the devil comes in like a flood.

My destination is charted and final and that is true

My only concern is when I get to heaven, will the sky still be blue?

A thousand may fall at my side when the economy collapses

Ten thousand may cringe when authorities integrity lapses.

Bad people will always haunt the world and feed on it's fears;

Driving people like herds of sheep this way and that.

The Bible says they have been doing that for years.

And they will keep doing it until the end and that's that.

So before you beat your plow into a sword,

Remember, you still have to tend the land.

It is hard to cultivate a field with a weapon,

Let God and the angels protect you, it is written in His plan.

King Solomon by Mary Agnes Smith

He is regal; everybody says or just acts like a little old man.

He'll look around when he is called but stubbornly he will stand

He looks at you with total shock. "you talkin' to me" he says.

I'm on my way, just wait a bit. Then he turns his head

He is on his own timetable. He will come when he is ready.

He knows you're there. He strolls along . . . slowly . . . but always steady.

He had big sister Bitsy but then she went to heaven.

He liked being top dog for a while, but he misses his companion

There's that gal next door but she's not Bitsy, Fieona is her name.

She comes and plays with him sometime

But it just isn't quite the same.

Then one day dad and mom said "let's go for a ride"

We know somewhere, where sisters live and we'll find one just your size",

"That's the one" the lady said "She's Scottish, Cairn mixed'"

Not sure about that Scottie part, but that hair cut had to be fixed.

He took her home to run and play where he'll be her big brother.

The yard is big with lots of toys. A place to share with one another.

Like any king upon his throne, Solomon is no different.

He still patrols his kingdom, but now with an assistant.

Knights of the Road by William Lynn Smith

Knights of the road? You don't see them much anymore
Oh, every once and a while one comes to my back door.
Once they knock, they keep their distance.
With hat in hand, and without insistence,
They don't want money; though they won't turn it away.
It is food stuff they need; not the perishable kind, they say.
I checked over that door and sure enough I see,
Four dirty finger prints guiding the others to me.
You see, this is their sign that means that it's OK
To knock on this door; you won't be sent away.

There aren't as many now as when I was a young man,
Working on the railroad fulfilling my family's plan.
I would see them in the rail yards, waiting and killing time,
For that next fast freight going somewhere down the line.
They aren't particularly friendly, they don't trust anyone.
They live in the hobo jungles; a life not for everyone,
They might ask "Got a cigarette? Thanks. Which one's goin' west?"
As far as conversations go, that's pretty much their best.
They might ask about some rumor that they have heard;
Work was there in the oil fields of Texas was the recent word.
Just a bed roll or a tramp bag; always travelling free and light.
Their shoes always tied in knots before stopping for the night.
"Keeps 'em from getting took" was the answer to why.
"I needs my shoes to keep goin' 'cause I can't fly"
"I don't pack my clothes, I wears 'em; don't need no case"
"I'll take me a bath and warsh them when I finds me a base"

I knew I would not see him again, probably won't be back.
"Take it easy, old head. Do ya want the rest of the pack?"
They would always take it and say thanks for the smokes,
"If you're ever in my home town would you say hello to my folks".

You know, I sort of miss those encounters on the rails.

The bos were always good for the telling of a few good tales

But most of them are gone now; most cars are locked and sealed.

They've taken to the highways, away from the ribbons of steel.

The spirit is still there no matter where they go

It takes a special freedom to be a real hobo

Love by William Lynn Smith

What does the word "love" mean to you?
Is it the intimate act between two?
Is it holding hands and strolling in the night?
Does it mean reconciliation after a fight?

"Love" has many a varied meaning,
But toward a parent's love I'm leaning.
Love is caring for the helpless type,
Even when a nasty butt needs a wipe.
Love is holding a sick ones head,
And changing the sheets on the sick bed.
Love is wrapping an arm around the shoulder,
Of a new driver that just rammed a boulder.
Love is not sitting in judgment strict
When a check book has been left derelict.
Love is listening with pride and rapt awe
When the music really sounds like a warped saw.

Love is hurting when a loved one falls
Love is working hard for your folks in your overalls
Love is listening patiently without speaking.
Love is fixing (without being asked) something that is squeaking
Love is complimenting because she looks so sweet.
Love is never keeping an emotion balance sheet.

God's Word said it best with these verses that do not rhyme.

I Corinthians 13:4–8

Love suffers long and is kind; love does not envy; love does not parade itself, is not puffed up. Does not behave rudely, does not seek its own, is not provoked and thinks no evil; does not rejoice in iniquity, but rejoices in the truth; bears all things, believes all things, hopes all things, endures all things; love never fails . . . .
Holy Bible New King James Version

That pretty much sums up what I believe love is;

I'm sure you can see I feel it is much more than a kiss.

The bottom line on love is that God did not consider it a loss,

To love us so much that he would die for us on a cross.

Masks by William Lynn Smith

Today I learned a lesson from my granddaughter's speech;
She was chosen to give a talk for her senior class chapel
I thought it would be the standard talk on "world peace"
Or some medical description about the dangers of a scalpel.
Turns out she had a great deal of courage to stand and ask;
How many of us in the room routinely wear a mask?
Not the kind that's worn on Mardi gras or at Halloween
But the subtle kind of mask that keeps us hidden and unseen
Because we are basically afraid to face others as we are,
We wear masks that conceal our fears, hurts and scars.

Uh, I looked around; that one came out of left field.
Her mom and dad were stoic, no emotion did they yield
She continued describing her life from age seven until now
Her words had the aim of a rifle and the finesse of a snow plow.
Having to live in two homes was the bane of her existence,
Being shared by two people like a property or a line fence.
Being in the middle, not mediating but a go-between
Not trusting either parent; having to keep her wits keen.
Because no matter what she said, spoke or related
It was always interpreted wrong by the partner hated.

So she put on a mask, a simple one to learn;
A carefree teenage girl showing little concern.
It was easier to do that than face up to all the crap.
That life and all those in it were dumping in her lap.
One of our biggest problems with wearing a mask
Is the trust that we have for each other becomes a task.
"I can't trust in you because I am afraid you'll hurt me.
So I'll keep my distance and my options to stay free."

The point of her oration was that our masks keep us slaves
To the fantasy world we create and how we must behave.
Jesus had two commands that he gave us before he left;
"Spread the Gospel and love others as you love yourself"
He also told us to always live in truth; in life that is the key.
Because if you have the truth, "the truth shall set you free"

After the festivities and the kids were going back to class,
I watched my granddaughter as she and her friends walked past.
In life I know she has had a pretty rocky start,
But her powerful speech touched this old railroader's heart.

Mister Lidge by William Lynn Smith

Some of my first memories were about that little church we attended
The kind of place a feller could go in his overalls without being offended.
The piano was off key and the hymnals were a little threadbare.
But even back then I knew that the Holy Spirit really lived there.
The pews were old but comfortable, the sanctuary had a stove in the middle
In the winter we would gather to worship and shiver just a little.

Mister Lidge was always there; sitting in the very front pew.
He was stooped and had wispy silver hair that numbered just a few.
I remember the suit that he wore; it was black and shiny in places
His shoes were worn but always shined and always had new laces.
These were the kinds of things a little boy was sure to see.
That old man never knew it but he meant a bunch to me.

It didn't matter what song the congregation would sing

Mister Lidge would lean forward and let his voice ring.

But even then I knew that his singing was almost amusing

All he did was shouting; and it was never in time with the music.

From the perspective of a kid, Mister Lidge was just part of the scenery

You know, like things that never change; the furniture and greenery.

He wasn't funny or even sad to me;

he just was and tha's all he would ever be.

As I grew older and we moved away from the home place

My perspective changed as did the situations I would face

Mister Lidge was older too; his suit shirt was showing stain blots

His shoes were scuffed; the laces were broken and tied in knots

His hair was lighter and thinner; more like spun silver thread

There were liver spots and moles appearing on his head.

He was certainly not cool like me with my Beatle boots and long hair.

As a teenager in the '60s I just really didn't want to be there.

Mister Lidge's singing was just noise; an embarrassment to me.

I wish I could go back; change my behavior; his sweet old face to see.

You see, now I am the old man that is struggling with singing and life.

I have worn out ten automobiles, two motorcycles and out lived one wife.

I know I embarrass my teenage grandchildren; my ways they don't understand.

Kind of like the guy enjoying the dance until someone stepped on his hand.

Now and then Mister Lidge comes to my mind softly like his wispy hair

Usually when I hit a sour note in the choir or reflecting in my reclining chair

I visualize our meeting when I make heaven's gate at last.

How family and friends who've gone before will greet me as I pass.

I am ushered into a concert hall grander than anything on earth

Seated in opulent cushions on a chair of incalculable worth,

Heavens choir of the angelic hosts sing, in perfect harmony

My heart swells as the music comes in symphonic mastery.

The maestro's conducting was masterful and flowing.

He had a real familiar face, one I vaguely remember knowing

With silver hair and sweet smiling face;

Mister Lidge had finally taken his rightful place.

Momma by William Lynn Smith

When I first met my momma it was not under the best of conditions.
I was nothing but a big ol' pain and she felt that she had been sent to perdition.
She birthed a half grown kid, twelve pounds fifteen ounces and squallin,
I'm sure that if the truth was told; a few names my daddy she was callin'
But we came through it together she had a brand new baby boy.
She knew that he was going to be a handful and not a mere toy.
Pain was not new for momma either physical or in the spirit.
She gathered herself up, took a hold and just dealt with it.
You know, her toughness is not really surprising once it was told to me
What her family's origin was, where they lived and how they came to be.

She sent my dad off to war and she stayed home to raise a son and make a living
She never complained; just made it work; stayed at it and kept on giving.
Like all her folks, she came from the toughest highlander stock
She was tough as leather, smooth as silk and steady as a rock.
I've heard it said that God will not give us more than we can bear
Momma must have the capacity of a diesel truck considering her load of care.
After daddy came home like a million other GIs to no jobs or money
They worked to make a living and did whatever it took make a family
Just when it looked like there was light at the end of the tunnel lane
It turned out that what they were seeing was just another train.
Dad had an accident that put him in the hospital for two years
I am sure momma had a hard time distinguishing between sweat and tears.
Like always with grit and determination she held our family tightly together
Doing whatever it took, driving a truck, making a crop; in all kinds of weather.
Daddy came home and momma nursed him back to health
We were all together again and that was better than any wealth.

I remember one incident that occurred when she stepped off the bus from work.
I was being chased by some boys that were screaming "C'mere you jerk".
She stopped me and asked what is going on; I said they wanted to fight.
"All of them?" She asked. She looked at the boys and said "Is that right?"

"Yeah, he called my brother a name" Glen hissed "on his butt we're gonna climb"
She said "If you want to fight him, and I'm not sure why, you'll do it one at a time"
"He is going to whip each one of you, I am sure of that, you see.
"Because if he doesn't, he is going to get a real whipping from me.
I remember fighting for my life and sent all those clowns to pack
It was the first of many days that I knew my momma had my back.

Momma has been my inspiration; some things could not have been worse.
Like the time my sister totaled the family car; in a parking lot; in reverse.
Then there was the time we all had intestinal flu or dysentery
Seven people in a little house with only one bathroom . . . scary.
But momma always came through and took us with her no matter how far.
She practiced "no child left behind" a long time before it was popular.

Well, it has been a long and exciting ride but now it's time to slow down
Daddy has gone on; most of us have moved and are no longer around.
No matter how old I get, no matter how many glories
I still see my momma everyday in my fondest memories.
The times on the back porch; in the rinse water; she would take me to dunk.
There was the time she let Wanda, Ann and me out of a locked automobile trunk
There were the times that she would be gripped with paralyzing fear
She would scream for Jesse to kill any little ol' snake would come near.
She also grabbed up a severely injured child when the blood flowed.
Wrapped his arm in a freshly washed sheet and ran for the road.

My momma is a rather remarkable lady.

My Brother Jesse by William Lynn Smith (baby)

Jesse never had a real childhood, not like my sister and me.

Right after he was born our dad had to go and fight a war across the sea.

Before he left, Daddy looked down in the crib where Jesse lay sleeping

"While daddy's gone you will be the man, my place you'll be keeping.

"Well, take care of the place and take good care of your mother".

Dad left Western Valley, fought a war and tearfully buried a brother

Jesse never was a baby or a toddler, he wasn't given the time.

Paw, our grandfather, loved him and treated him like a son, part of the line.

Instead of playing with blocks and toys around the house all day,

He followed his paw, learned to work hard, and how to hate bales of hay.

Above all things he wanted to do, his first love was taking care of his mother.

And he did.

Dad came home like a million others and wanted to start his life anew.

Jesse just looked at the guy in the soldier suit and said "who the heck are you?"

Adjustment for him was pretty hard. First it was one thing then another,

But it was dad's affection for mom that tore it, "Take your hands off my mother!"

Finally the peace was made and Jess realized that the guy was his loving dad

His place as head of the house had been reclaimed and that wasn't half bad.

Even though dad was back, Jess still couldn't be just a kid

He had chores to be done around the place, all of which he did.

He was there for the birth of Wanda now he added nurse maid to his time.

He had to help mother with the baby, the bottles and the clothes on the line.

That was a pretty good load for a kid that was only four years old.

I am sure he missed being the only one a little, if the truth could be told.

Things were settling down when Jesse was close to eight

Then along came half grown William bolting through the gate.

Now his joy was multiplied by two and on top of that he had a little brother

At last there will be some others to help him take care of his mother.

And they did.

When he was nine, his path in life would have grief that must be shared

Daddy was burned horribly in a truck accident but his life was spared.

Here was a kid barely old enough to see over the wheel

Having the weight of the world on him, how alone he must feel.

Mom would spend days, months and even years

In the hospital with dad till she had no more tears.

Dad was lying on greased sheets with hoses first this way and the other.

He looked at Jesse—"take care of the place and take good care of your mother".

And he did.

He worked with the other men on the farm, took daddy's place every day.

He raised pigs in the bottom, pulled corn, picked cotton and bailed hay

He didn't have time to play like we did but I never heard him complain

He was always responsible, worked real hard even when it was a pain.

Eventually when dad got out of the hospital, Jesse was almost eleven years old

He was operating tractors, combines; driving trucks and cars I've been told.

By this time he had developed the habit of working and making his own way.

He had an independent spirit; he had his own mind and certainly his own say.

I guess that is why Jesse was more of an authority figure to me at first

He didn't play nasty tricks on me like my cousins did, sometime he was worse.

"Note to self" never expect Jess to help hide a failing grade in school.

He'd always rat me out to mom and I never thought that was cool.

We gave Jess a bum rap, claimed he was a perfectionist and really mean
He just had no time for our whining about our rooms we had to clean.
I was the baby and I'm sure he loved me . . . some. He even loved Wanda when she
Would do weird stupid stuff and then scream "you're not the boss of me!"

He saved money, left home, grew up some and married the love of his life
When he met a lovely stewardess named Carol and took her as his wife
They were two of a kind, he and she,
Both the oldest and full of responsibility.
Their lives are full of fun, work and travel that they do gaily;
They kept their words to their families and care for them daily.
I have to laugh when someone says, they're selfish; they just don't care.
Because they never had kids so their lives they could share.
Oh come on now. First there was little sister Wanda and then there was me.
Jesse has already shared with enough kids that kept his life from being free.
Besides when mom and dad had company, it was Jesse's bed that was given.
He was relegated to the floor on a pallet in the room we used for livin'
But I have to give them credit because Nancy and Aunt Carol had a plan form.
Nancy's part was to have the "experimental" child to work with so Jyll was born.
From that point the way they shared their lives was all up to fate
Their nieces and nephews number approximately eight.
They were asked to take care of the children even though that had none.
And they did.

Now it is time to close and most of the first generation is gone
Dad was in his death bed waiting to be called and go on home.
He looked 'round the room from one face and then the other
He said to Jess, "Take care of the place and take good care of your mother".
And he did

My Favorite Time of Day

by William Lynn Smith

My favorite time of the day? Please don't think it odd;

It's early in the morning when it is just me and God.

You know, for a supreme being He is really an OK Guy

He just listens intently to me and never asks "Why?"

I can clean out the garbage from my mind and my heart.

He helps me go through it; we sort it out from the start.

He is always there for me no matter what time of day;

Even if everyone else just leaves me, he will always stay.

I don't really remember ever walking through the place of the curse,

But I've been places on the railroad that seemed much, much worse.

Some of my friends and relatives may want to know for sure

How can we go through this life with the sadness we must endure?

"William, how do you know that God is real?" they just up and ask it.

My proof is simple: I'm here, healthy, happy and not in a casket.

My Guardian by William Lynn Smith

The silent darkness envelopes me with its soft embrace,
I become detached from the realities I face;
Another day has come and gone,
And I lay here alone;
To sleep.

During the night I know that I am safe; without fear of harm.
My sleep is sweet; my head lies lightly on my arm;
An angelic being stands close by;
Alert for any alarm or cry;
My guardian.

The Holy Spirit has placed her there with orders to watch over me;
She spans spirit and temporal, a strong and quiet sentry.
Meeting all manner of threats and danger;
With unwavering demeanor;
My guardian.

One night or day when the trumpet of God is blown to retrieve his children
I know I will be in the happy throngs of souls that he has bidden.
Trading my old tired body for a glorious new one,
Heading toward heaven at a dead run.
With my guardian.

My Motorcycle By William Lynn Smith

Some people think I am crazy but I know what I like

It is just that some days I love riding on my bike.

I drop myself on that big ol' seat of leather

Fire up that six cylinder and feel light as a feather

I am no Peter Fonda or a Hell's Angel wannabe

I'm just Will Ordinary with a need to be a little free.

It has Illusion Blue paint and chrome everything else

It has all the amenities; all the whistles and the bells.

I don't wear a do rag with leather vest and pack;

I don't want some half naked lot lizard hanging on my back.

I don't wear tattoo sleeves so my arms will look like anarchy

In fact I don't believe in that "rebel without a cause" malarkey

My bike is a civilized Gold Wing with smooth and quiet power.

It won't shake your arms off if you ride more than an hour.

I'm not an outlaw; I don't showboat, or rawhide my machine;

I know it'll go fast enough; I don't have to show that it's mean.

Besides when you are my age and you have an awful lot to lose,

You ride for yourself and your experience; there's nothing else to prove.

I will let the weekend fair weather riders act like the biker bum lot;
With leather jackets, designer ragged jeans and leaking oil spots.

Nope, this scooter is just for our enjoyment, my Mary and me;
Life is too short to be old; we have found that happiness is the key
We ride when we want to or just sit around and look really cool;
We laugh at the frowning prudes when they say, "look at those old fools"
Because we know a secret that they don't want to be told;
They'd like to do the same thing we do, but they just aren't that bold.

My Sister, Wanda By William Lynn Smith

My sister Wanda is a wonderful woman and a beautiful lady,
She is a country girl that became cosmopolitan and not a bit shady
To begin with she was thrust fanny first into this life,
A sight to behold; folded in half like a big ol' jack knife
Her ankles were firmly placed behind her sweet little head
She couldn't be left alone because she might roll off her bed.
From her life we learned miracles are not always from above.
All miracles are from God; some involve a pillow and a mother's love
An invalid's life was not going to be accepted for momma's new baby.
She was going to make it right no matter what; she didn't mean maybe.
She worked with those little legs, hips and feet;
Using a pillow and its case to unfold her on the sheet.
Over and over she rubbed and caressed that baby's legs
At long last they were stronger and straighter than pegs

Wanda grew and became the apple of dad's eye.
She was one of only two girls that mattered in his life
However, she had a somewhat ornery and hard headed streak.
And if you crossed her, your chances of survival were bleak.
She would get mad at my brother then come pound me good.
That is why, during their arguments, I was real careful where I stood.
She was the middle child and caught it from both ends
Jesse would boss her around; I was the baby; no friends.
We were country kids, some of us worked but all of us always played hard.
There was no air conditioning or TV in the house so we stayed in the yard.
Tag, mule biscuit fights, building twine bridges over gullies or just hiding out.
Wanda could take any of our cousins two out of three falls in a bout.
She could out spit, out fight and out run all of us and I can tell you for sure
She had a mean way with a hammer or brick; a smart mouth to cure.
Her independent spirit was strong and served her well as she grew.
Except a couple of times she should have come home because she knew
Momma was there waiting for her and it was way after dark

Finally she would send Jesse to get her from her friends at the park.

You could hear them coming up Seventh Street just a yelling

Jesse herding her from behind and to him she was telling

"You're not the boss of me, I'll go home when I am ready, dimwit"

However momma's patience had been stretched past the limit.

Needless to say Wanda received another life lesson on being prompt.

It didn't dampen her spirit, not a bit; the next day to the park she romped.

The last time Wanda stayed out late was when daddy came home from a trip.

Momma said "J.W. she will not come home and gives Jesse a bunch of lip"

Daddy left the yard and walked slowly, like an executioner, toward the park

I watched closely as usual but I lost sight of him as he disappeared into the dark.

It wasn't long before we heard Wanda coming back wailing and cryin'

Instead of a little girl, she sounded more like a civil defense air-raid siren.

When she went to Humes high school and met the teachers there

They all expected her to be just like Jesse except with a female flair.

Man, were they surprised when Wanda turned out to be

Her own girl, not like Jess at all; then there was me.

(but that is another story that probably should just go by)

Wanda finished high school and gave college a little try.

Jesse got married and we all had a good time celebrating'

I found it ain't a good thing to try and jump-start her car you're berating.

After that, a stint with the First National Bank was put on her resume'

'Till at last she landed a job at Delta Air Lines and just flew away.

She always was close to the family no matter where she was based

She worked with Delta to allow dad and mom to fly all over the place.

Even though she dated a bunch of fellas and was quite the catch,

She must have been Teflon coated because there was no place a guy could latch.

She was in the rough and tumble world of passenger airlines learning how it feels

To be serving on a bucking aisle way backwards in a tight skirt and high heels.

Charli was her very closest friend and one of the premier Delta stews.

They travelled everywhere; even on safari in Africa to take in the views.

They crawled over the fence in the compound to get a closer look at wildlife,

They had no protection with them; no guide, no gun not even a pen knife.

The guard alerted the guide that some tourists had left the enclosure

The guide had to make sure they were rescued from the danger exposure.
After it was done and the two stews were safe, he wanted them stifled
"Don't worry, ma'am. It wasn't the lions were going to shoot with our rifles."

Eventually Wanda wanted to slow down a little and get real domestic.
She married a Mississippi boy, lived in Texas and life was good but hectic.
She and Randy adopted two clowns (I guess starting a circus was on their mind)
But that's a whole 'nother story we won't go into now; I don't have the time.
She fulfilled a promise she made and provided a home for mom and dad.
Life with them on the Tennessee hills in a small town wasn't half bad.

Daddy was called to Jesus; he took his seat beside Paw at the heavenly feast.
It was a bitter sweet time; we would miss him, but his awful pain had ceased.
Momma, Jesse, Wanda and I committed his body to the warm Tennessee soil.
A fitting place for this a giant of a man; a father resting from his life's toil.
Wanda was there like she always was in times that were fat or slim
Even when daddy's little helper, my Nancy, went on ahead to be with him.
It was times that like that when life is wrecked like a trailer park in a twister.
It is wonderful to have a good family but nothing beats a loving sister!

Not Alone by William Lynn Smith

In the Pacific Northwest lives the Children of the Forest
The tribe has a name but the knowledge of it can rest
It is enough to be said that they live at one with the earth
They are clans and families with relationships beyond worth
They have ways that may seem strange and foreign today
But they have lived and loved through all the ages this way.
From the womb to the grave each one cares for the other.
In the village every man is a father and every woman a mother.

There comes a time of testing as the boy becomes a man;
A rite of passage that proves his mettle in the clan.
The boy is given a knife and using the things he has learned;
He must go into the forest alone, a privilege he has earned.

The young man kisses his mother and takes a blessing from his father,
He saunters off toward the woods as the darkness begins to gather.
He goes deeper into the forest than he has ever ventured before,
to that place where monsters and spirits dwell, as told in tales of lore.
He finds a place to spend the night as the evening shadows fall,
he lays his blanket on the ground and hears the night birds call.

The night produces strange sounds that feed his darkest fear.
Was that a bear pushing through the brush or maybe just a deer?
Was that a raccoon chattering and scolding him in the night?
Was it some poor lost spirit calling to him, just beyond his sight?
The fear and darkness began to steal his youthful bravery.
It takes his freedom from him, and replaces it with frightened slavery.
All night he sits with his blanket wrapped around him tightly,
watching the forest from under the folds while shivering slightly.

At last the sky in the east begins to brighten with a rosy hue
The darkness retreats to the shadows, the forest drips with dew.
Across the clearing from him stands a figure that is not yet clear.
Is it an animal or a tree trunk that has a shape producing fear?

Finally the light has revealed a warrior standing straight and tall.

The young man jumped to his feet and stood ready to give his all.

The awesome warrior turns slightly to as if to face his foe,

His arms out stretched toward the young man, he didn't draw his bow.

He recognized the face of the brave he was about to meet.

It was his own father that he went forward to greet.

"My father, did you come out during the night to bring me home?"

"No my son I have stood guard over your camp while you slept alone."

"Father, do you shame me? Do you not believe that I can be a man?"

"How can I say that I have passed the test and be a brave in the clan?"

The old warrior's craggy face broke into a soft and tender smile.

He reached out for the young brave and held him for a while.

"My son, please don't be alarmed or angry, for I know how you feel."

"Like all braves, you have spent this night learning that fear is not real"

"My father guarded me like I have guarded you this night,

To keep real danger from you while you defeat your fear and fright."

The young brave learned the lesson that the other braves have known

No matter how bad the situation is they face they are never really alone.

We can learn a lesson from the children of the forest.

That no matter where we are in life our God is always with us.

Though our earthly fathers may not keep us all from harm

Our heavenly Father is always near, holding us in his loving arms.

Our Maggie Mae by Mary Agnes Smith

Scottish? No. Carin? No. A Bushland, that's our Maggie
With crazy hair that looks like hay.
She is really kind of shaggy.
We went to check her out one day,
She really was a mess.
They'd clipped her hair and though quite cute
She looked a bit distressed.
She won our hearts and home she came,
To be our Sollies sister
Don't let that sweet face fool you, though
She's like a Texas twister.
She's Maggie and Maggie Mae and sometimes even MARGARET!!
But when she chases the squirrels away
She is always right on target!
She steals your heart and runs away
And jumps up in your chair.
But really, she only wants to play
And the chair is there to share.

With big round eyes and a little nose she looks like a baby seal.

Especially when she misbehaves, your anger they will steal.

Her ears are trimmed with feather hair.

They just complete her look,

A picture of our Maggie you won't find in any book.

She loves to run and play outside,

Which she does with so much charm.

But 9 o'clock, "let's go to bed," she sleeps under daddy's arm.

Problems by William Lynn Smith

What? Oh, don't tell me your problems please.

You see I'm not equipped to handle these.

Yes, I'm sorry about your miserable plight,

But you should know it isn't me that can make it right.

Of course I can help with something heavy or loan you a tool,

But if you depend on me for more than that you'll look like a fool.

Hey, don't go away. What I can do, to be fair and kind of nice.

To help you in the future I can offer you some really valuable advice.

If a machine that you own blows up and does everything but bleed,

Go to the source and get out the owner's manual before you proceed.

The same can be said about this life that we are living

Hey, listen here, you asked for this advice that I'm giving!

You've done all you can but just face the fact: life just isn't always fair.

When you're at the end of your rope, tie a knot in it and just hang in there

When bad stuff happens, times are tough and you feel like a heel

Don't go whining to others, go to the source, don't forget to kneel.

If you'll reach out for God, He will reach out and hold you.

Just learn to listen; His voice is not always from the blue.

When you are at the bottom of the deepest pit of darkest despair,

Remember, God's Word says "don't worry, I will also be there".

If you need it He will even let you wear His armor, that's true.

Then nothing hurts no matter what the devil throws at you.

Just a little more advice I can offer if you care to listen to me.

Keep a copy of His manual, the Bible, close by. His advice is free.

Oh yeah, one more thing you should know before I leave you here.

Just remember these facts and you should have no cause to fear.

He said he will be with you in the valley or on the mount.

That means **you** must decide to go and then **you** must step out.

He will walk beside you taking care of all your problems and strife

But that makes a lot more sense if you are doing what **He** wills in your life.

Puddles by William Lynn Smith

Did you ever notice the puddles left after the rain?
You have to step around them now and then.
You do that because wet shoes are a real pain;
they leave tracks showing where you've been.
Puddles can also pose a real danger there
Because if you don't watch where you step,
You'll slip and fall causing your anger to flair.
Knowing you should've looked before you leapt.

I believe that life is like a coffee cup,
God's blessings filling it, and running over.
We know that we can't use it up,
So we should bless others with what fell over.
If we're not good stewards of all that he has given us,
And we try to hoard it, not sharing with our brothers.
The puddles of blessings will eventually drown us.
While we're guarding our stuff and not helping others.

Sadness by William Lynn Smith

It is quiet and still when sadness comes to visit,
In my favorite time when I write with humor and wit.
The early morning visitor it is not very good company
It brings the dark thoughts that have come for me.
It wraps itself around me like a worn out ragged sheet;
I have to be careful with this one, like crossing a street.
The battle is joined.

With each thought that arrives the sadness in heart grows,
like a mold that will eventually effect what my mind knows.
It grows and proceeds; pushing away my pleasant thoughts,
Replacing them with darkness; bringing my day to naught.
'Till at last I simply stop and hand over the control of the day
To the sadness that has replaced my happiness in this way,
The battle is lost.

Today I will do it differently; I will call on Jesus in my quiet time.
When the sadness shows up to stay, WE will simply draw the line.
My heart's station will be closed when the sadness express arrives
The dark thoughts will not be allowed; no matter how they strive.
When I begin to think about a lousy day or what I have been told,
I will say a breath prayer, take God's light and kill out the mold.
Without a beginning the sadness will not have any say
About what I feel, how I act, or how I will spend my day.
Without dwelling on the dark thoughts or nursing some little grudge
My mind is free to work on good things like an easy recipe for fudge.
I can think about and work on helping someone who has a need;
Rather than worrying about what's in it for me; you know that's greed.
With God's light all around there is no place for sin and evil to hide,
With God's light on the path I am taking, I will not need a guide.
This day is great; there is a lot to do and when it is all done,
I will end my day with prayer for the VICTORY God has won!

Sitting Quietly by William Lynn Smith

The day is just starting and I am fresh with a bunch of "want tos"
Trying to plan out my time and effort against a list of "need tos"
The coffee in my cup is warm and comforting as the steam rises.
I pull God's armor on; getting ready for all of life's surprises.
After reading the Ninety First Psalm
from the Bible I have in my palm,
I just sit quietly.

The time is progressing and the plans we made are coming together well,
The "need tos" are being addressed and a few of the "want tos" as well.
I wipe the grease from my hands as I watch my wife across the room.
She is such a prize; a friend, a coach, she is womanhood in full bloom.
My body is yielding to a good fatigue.
My effort and the time are in league.
To say a short breath prayer finally,
I just sit quietly.

The sun is setting and the day has been spent well. My tools are laid aside.
We are closing down work, cleaning up the area. It is time to go on inside.
The meal is prepared and eaten with quiet conversation and enjoyment
The dishes are washed, dried and put away after their employment.
We go and turn on the TV and see what the world has to say.
After a while we turn it off and make the world go away.
Turn back the bed and prepare for the night.
Say my prayers; turn out the light.
Savoring the victory of the fight
reflecting life's finality,
I just lay quietly

Day in, day out; keep on keeping on; that is how it is done.

Life ain't that complicated cause you are the only one

To decide what you will do with the day,

How you will act; what you will say.

Trust in His armor with your life, to

always keep you safe from strife.

'till at last, you're through.

Life is done with you;

Your soul is freed,

Your body is laid

Quietly.

The Boy From Western Valley

by William Lynn Smith

On a bench in Wincanton, England he stared out over the Salisbury Plain.
He reflected on how he got here. Would he ever see home again?
Would he ever hold his new young wife or bounce his beautiful son on his knee?
How he longed to fish or hunt birds in the bottoms along the Loosahatchie.
But right now he and Big'un had a job to do just like when logging for Paw.
Just reach and get it and hold on tight; ride it until you're raw.
They sent us over here to end this fight so these folks can have law.

He mounted the cab of his Reo deuce and a half and trundled off toward the station.
It was his job to meet the train and get the mail for his buddy's jubilation.
He parked his rig at the curb on the street out front by the milk cans.
Leaned against the truck and pulled a sandwich from the pocket of his pants.
A lady he had seen and spoke to before with her daughter was standing near.
He looked down at the wax paper covered sandwich and wished he had a beer.
"Good mornin' yank" she said with a smile. The little girl hid behind her skirt.
"Yes ma'am it is at that" he said with a grin "and how's that little squirt?"
"We're good" she answered "Hopefully there will be news of James on the train"
"You know he's still in North Africa these many months" her face showing the pain.

The pain of being away from her loved one, hoping against hope to see him again.

"I'm sure that he is all right." He replied. "You gals hungry? Care for some canned ham?"

"Oh that would be wonderful and I tell you what we would like to do.

We will bring you a Welsh rabbit tomorrow." She said and he began to think—STEW!

The next day he got his Welsh rabbit from her and thought "Man this is really rich."

I told all the guys at the camp about rabbit stew and now I just have this cheese sandwich.

The next weeks were a blur of excitement, hard work and the anxiety of pending battle.

Of loading trucks, slinging crates on cranes, loading ships and hearing the tackle rattle.

They were all pretty much wet and miserable, knowing their fate was a chance.

Waiting for the word to proceed and begin the final move on to France.

D-day finally came; the landing crafts were loaded, they headed for the land.

Men wading from the Higgins boats to the shore, valor and death walking hand in hand.

With bravery, tears and hard work our victory was attained

The plan had worked, the men had done the job and a foot hold was gained.

Now it was the time for the medics and supply guys with trucks, to help the army move.

They moved supplies forward and the wounded back, tread marks in the muddy track.

The work was hard but it was worth it to keep the guys moving on ahead.

Battle tanks and trucks slogging along the fields and hedge rows bordered with the dead.

When time came rest and his truck was pulled to the side, he slept in dog tired fits

It was uncomfortable in the cargo bed, but compared to the other resting places it was the Ritz.

Then there was the hour that the chaplain came and asked "Are you Private Jesse W. Smith?"

"I am" he said then the chaplain continued "I am afraid I have bad news about you brother, Wesley"

"He was killed in action on a field not far from here. The result of the sniper's aim was deadly"

The boy from Western Valley felt the whole world crashing down. Time had come untethered.

Big'un was his older brother, his best friend, they had been though it all together.

The chaplain said a prayer to God and no one there thought it was odd to see grown men cry;

His brother gave it all, paid the debt in full never really understanding why.

They had selected a farmer's field just off the road to lay their warriors to rest.

The boy from Western Valley watched the line of stretchers containing America's best.

The chaplains prayed over each one, as they gently laid them beneath the clover.

"Don't worry, son." The chaplain said. "We'll bring him home as soon as this is over."

The boy stood up and brushed his knees. Wiping Normandy's dirt from his hands.

He always knew that death was real but hadn't reckoned it on foreign lands.

From that point he went on; He and about a million other American GIs

He drove that deuce and a half all the way to Berlin and silenced Hitler's lies.

At last the people of France were free; they danced in the streets in victory.

He swung down from the bed of the truck that beautiful West Tennessee day.

She ran to greet him carrying his son to meet him, to hear what he had to say.

It was some time later, in a cold November. They unloaded Bigun from the train

He was one of thousands of sons, dads and brothers arriving home again.

After he was buried and the man gave Paw our flag, Wesley was no longer alone.

Because all the boys from Western Valley had finally come home.

The Dream by William Lynn Smith

In a dream I was walking along a path, shaded and pleasant
Restful woodland sounds and an occasional startled pheasant
I came to a clearing, the edge of a neat little group of dwellings
One in particular caught my attention because of the yelling
A man and woman, I took to be husband and wife, were really quite loud.
In fact it was so much so they were drawing a real crowd.

As I stood and watched somewhat amused by their antics
It became clear that things were getting worse, they were becoming more frantic.
He was ripping shingles off the roof and throwing them down
She was pulling the shutters off the windows, leaving them on the ground
Together they were making the neat little cottage look like a pile of rubble
All the while screaming and yelling at each other promoting the trouble.

In the crowd I happened to notice a man standing close by
So I walked across the way and asked him if he knew why
Oh, they are suffering from a malady that is common in these parts,
It is a virus, I think, that causes the separation of the hearts.
It always happens to the married couples and starts simply enough
The origin is a mystery, but they are usually infected by their stuff.
The symptoms although unique to the person are mostly the same.
Missteps here, a little white lie there, excuses given are usually lame.
As the disease progresses and weaves itself into their life strands.
They no longer speak in the same language and neither understands.
Nothing he can say will ever comfort her and dry her tears.
She can't make him understand her concerns and her fears.
Until at last they begin to destroy the little house they built together.
Leaving the wreckage along with their dreams lying about in the weather.

Quite alarmed and transfixed I watched this hideous display

"I don't understand this at all, does it always end this way?"

"Not always" he said. "Sometimes another force gives the virus rout."

He pointed toward the clearing and I saw a gentle man step out.

"That's Jesus" the man beamed "He'll take care of this mess"

"Watch, He will fix their problems and love them both never the less"

The man and woman stopped their yelling and watched Jesus approach.

They moved toward Jesus and began to talk together without reproach.

I watched in awe as all three of them sat down in the grass.

Like kids in a school room, they were attentive as good ones in class.

"It works like this every time" the man said with a smile

He looked at me and said "You ought to talk to him once and a while".

The Road by William Lynn Smith

Sometimes I wonder where the road goes:
As it goes round a curve out sight.
How the grass in the ditch glows,
In the red from the cars tail lights.
The road is bordered by gravel on the ground.
The construction of it is concrete, gray and sturdy.
It is lined by tall bushes and grass turned brown.
Littered with waste cotton blown and dirty.

The road of my life is seen more clearly in the mirror.
Reflecting the places I have already past.
Some of those places I approached with fear,
But I arrived, faced them and won out at last.

I know where my road is going; with God that's sure.
I'm looking forward to the places I will see between here and there
That gift gives me a lot of happiness clean and pure;
I am not about to just stop and sit here; I'll get nowhere.
OK, I will keep moving along; That's best, I suppose.
But since my retirement I tend to stop more often,
To think about my God's work and smell His rose,
Before they place my worn out body in the coffin.

The Witness of a Christian

by William Lynn Smith

How do we spread the Gospel like Jesus commanded us to do?

I think because He made us all unique, that's really up to you.

Some of us are comfortable taking the Gospel to the beach,

But others of us will do the impossible, the lost souls to reach.

I have learned after traveling a great length down this highway of life

As Christians we will encounter several issues that can cause us strife.

First; inform your face that you are happy in the Lord.

This is the first indication that you have His spiritual sword.

We must remember that our face is the mirror of our soul,

And I don't know of anyone who is attracted to a dark dour hole.

Second; stroll confidently through your day, happy; quit hobblin'

That's easy if you stop telling everybody about your own problems.

It is hard for a person new to you that doesn't know about God,

To believe after hearing about your situations; makes that kind of odd.

Third; be a good example of the scripture that says "God will provide"

Don't just sit there like you're waiting for Him to come carry you for a ride.

Nothing keeps the lost more lost and hard for the Lord to retrieve,

Than folks who seem so phony and say things they don't really believe.

If you show that you really believe "The Lord will provide" put legs on that belief;

Don't let your laziness keep you from taking another soul from Satan like a thief

Next; if we are to attract the lost into the Kingdom we show them how.

To live good we must make it more attractive and not be "Holier than thou".

How can you expect them to make a decision that will affect the rest of their lives;

When your actions seem to accuse them of having infectious brain hives?

You see, it is much easier for them if we give a good example to hold,
If we open our arms as if to hug and not simply our hands to fold.
If we look closely at Jesus' words; that we should spread the Gospel
It looks like it is more of a task of refinement for us, as far as I can tell.
I thank my God every day for the opportunity to witness for Him,
Even for the soldiers dying on foreign soil for that freedom.
I will praise Him and honor them every day for that amazing chance
To be the Christian that I am known to be and firmly take my stance.

Under the Bridge by William Lynn Smith

The Lancaster Street Bridge under I35 W, just a little east of Main
There are folks staying under that bridge out of the sun and the rain
When you drive by them they look back with a certain blankness.
You know, the folks standing around with their stuff rolled in blankets.
You can call them homeless, knights of the road or just bums;
They come from good families, broken homes, suburbia or the slums.
They are all unique, but one thing they all have in common
Lancaster Street is where they stepped off life and landed on.

To be sure, most of them are there from the choices they have made;
The reasons they came are varied but out of necessity they stayed.
What can we do to help them? How can we make a change?
Not a whole lot really. It is from their past they made the exchange.
The Bible tells us not to "sing songs to a heavy heart", that's true.
"One size fits all" responses to their problems we know will not do.
We can't go all "holier than thou" to tell them what they did wrong.
They know why they are there; what they did; they have known it all along.

Jesus gave us the answer to the probing questions we ask.
He told His disciples that when He needed them, they passed.
He said that when He was hungry, they would not feed Him,
When He was tired and cold they would not comfort Him.
They stood aghast at His accusations; genuinely dismayed.
They loved Him; How could such callous acts be displayed?
"Lord, when did we see You hungry and cold and not react?"
"Where was this place where we did not honor our pact?"
He smiled, with a patience of a loving father when he spoke,
"If you didn't care for the least of them, My heart you broke"

This is just as true today; we need to simply and genuinely care.

Even though we cannot do everything for everyone there,

Make it count; do what we know in our hearts we can do;

A blanket, some effort; maybe some money too.

Will that make a difference? You bet!

Because Jesus and you don't forget.

Walls by William Lynn Smith

All of us build walls our whole lives through;
Not out of wood and stone but out of what we do.
Some of us build walls for our protection;
But mostly our walls are built for selection.
Our life's experiences we use for the brick.
Good or bad, the strong ones we always pick.
"Oh, I don't do that" I hear you say;
Really? Are your sure that after one bad day,
That you didn't sigh "I'll never do that again"?
Maybe you said "Ain't going where I already been?"
Whether it's the cap stone or the foundation laid,
You're building a wall, both solid and staid.

How can we tell if the walls we've built in our life
Are good ones or bad, for protection or strife?
Here are some questions we should ask ourselves
Before we put our wall building efforts on the shelves.
Do we hide behind the walls from all others?
Do we use them to help protect our brothers?
Are the walls in your life built to keep out stuff,
As we stand on the parapets running our bluff?
Or are they used to channel thoughts correctly;
To teach others using our knowledge effectively?

Yep, I think the walls we build in our lives are a guide.
They line the streets in our mind that are nice and wide.
The walls of our experiences keep our efforts focused.
Indecision will not devour them like a bunch of locusts.
"Well, just how do we do that, Mister Wizard?" you ask.
"It seems like a simple description of a very tough task!"
Not really; in fact, we've had the instructions all along
To build our life's walls for good purposes, solid and strong.

Like any good beginning of a major construction project
Is consulting an extremely good carpenter and architect.
Because the description of a bad wall, I'm sure you can relate
Is one where the material used in the construction is hate.
Jesus instructed His disciples long ago and it's still true;
To "Forgive and to love one another as I have loved you"
When we do that we have love and patience without regret.
That means no hatred is used when we forgive and forget.

If we continue this process over and over, day after day
We will be a benefit to those around us to light the way.
Because the walls a Christian builds aren't built for sin:
They're not built to keep folks out; they're there to guide them in.

West Tennessee Wind by William Lynn Smith

The west Tennessee wind is like a naughty child,
It is sometimes quiet and sometimes wild.
As it races along the city street,
Lifting dust and throwing it on my feet.
At times it hides between the buildings there,
Then jumps out to surprise when you're unaware.
As the crowd waits on the station platform,
The wind moves quietly through them
But when each train passes the wind blows by like a storm.
Whipping them about like a parent disciplining their children.
'Til at last it settles and apologizes by caressing their faces
As it sees them off when they board the trains to far off places.

I have to believe the wind is sad as it brushes by windows closed
That we don't come out to play again running through the hanging clothes.
How we enjoyed running through the sheets that momma hung
How the linens brushed by our ears or grabbing our little bodies snug
You know how it sometimes wrapped around us like a cool summer hug.
If she came out, Momma would always catch us then call out to say
"Those sheets were clean! You kids go find another place to play"
That ol' wind would turn away just as if to say, "I told them to go away!"

I remember how the wind would precede us as we chased down the grassy glen
Racing and swirling, lilting and twirling throwing leaves high into the air
It impishly whispered to the trees making them sigh about the places it has been
It moved about from place to place rearranging the leaves and trash
Piling it in the clefts of hills and buildings like a hoarder with his stash

The gentle wind carries the seeds for the next crop of wild flowers
It is clear that from the mundane to the awesome are the limits of its powers.
Like a farmer planting and tending his section of the land
It'll then roil up in thunder storms making the mighty trees bend.

The playmate of my youth can be a fearsome force as well.
Making the lives of those crushed by it a horrible confusing hell.
God told us through His Son that, no matter how awesome the wind
We have the power through the Holy One to call for peace and an end.

What's Wrong with This Country

By William Lynn Smith

WARNING! This is a long, dark and cynical poem that will-

(a) *Amuse the intelligent*

(b) *Confuse the ignorant*

(c) *Abuse the insolent*

PLEASE CONTINUE READING AT YOUR OWN RISK;
SOME OF THE CONTENT MAY BE DEEMED INAPPROPRIATE AND
OFFENSIVE

What is wrong with this country? I will tell you what,

As a people the citizens of this country are a gullible lot.

Even though we are a Christian nation and have access to the Bible,

We'd rather to listen to some clown spouting a bunch of psycho-babble.

Even though the books in God's Word are quite clear,

We would rather hear any non-sense that tingles our ear.

In fact we will believe in any theory that comes down the pike,

As long as it is championed by some no-talent celebrity or the like.

The news casting networks on TV gives us the clarion call

To inform and give instructions to one and all.

What is the cause du jour? (That means cause of the day)

It is one group after another wanting to have their say.

"The number one killer on the road is alcohol" The talking head opines.

A poor soul is retrieved and trotted out in front of the lens and whines.

"He was always such a good boy; always cooperative with the cops in the tank"

"But it was that bad old alcohol that caused . . . . (Nightly news to fill in the blank)"

You know, I think with the exception of the New England alcohol flood

I never knew of a bottle of whiskey ever killed someone in cold blood.

In fact I don't believe that any alcoholic beverage has ever committed murder.

Well, there was a cask of moonshine that killed Jim when it fell from the girder.

Carey Nations had the right idea; let's attack alcohol with axes where it lives.
Stop the bums who make the stuff and let them know exactly what gives
Well ol' Carey came through. Her prohibition of booze became a reality
It showed how a popular cause can make us try to legislate morality
Our collective memory is very short. Let's say almost minimal
Prohibition did not stop the booze but made a whole bunch of rich criminals.
What about the car the alcohol was riding in when the folks were hurt?
After all it was the automobile's muscle that did the dirty work.
So we need a campaign to bring those awful smoke belching monsters in line.
We need to see if we can get another out-of-work celebrity to help us whine.

Commercial Break—"Here is a commercial about the show you are watching.
In case you have gone comatose and can't remember what show you're watching.
Followed by a well made ad that tell us we must drink to help our sociability,
We can hang out with friends and guzzle booze as long as we do it responsibly.
Then with pulse pounding music the automobile companies take their shot
Letting us know exactly which machine is really, really hot.

Back to your nightly news—(Unreality TV)

Then the bunch comes on that wants to push gun control on the gullible flock,
It is time for another celebrity and a slick talking head to present their shock.
The stage hands off camera trot out another poor soul looking all sad and hurt
It seems that some gamer moron got a gun and shot everything wearing a shirt.
"He was always such a good boy; always cooperative with the cops in the tank"
"But it was those bad old guns that caused . . . . (Nightly news to fill in the blank)"
"Guns kill more innocent people in this country than any other cause"
The talking head looks dead into the lens with a purposeful pause.
This makes me wonder; just what kind of guns should we be on the lookout for.
Then I remember, holy cow! There is a rifle underneath my bed on the floor
Could it be laying there putting together some sort of evil plan?
What if it teams up an angry bottle of booze, no one is safe again!
Will the Rifles and Pistols suddenly kick down our doors?
Shooting and pillaging leaving us bleeding spread eagled on the floors.
Should we be concerned that the different calibers would join forces?
We should get the ASPCA involved in case they start shooting horses.

In any case we must enact very stringent gun control laws for all.
Then we can control assault hammers, chainsaws, and even the military awls.
Yep, that is the ticket. We will make every criminal that wants a gun
Go through an extensive background check. That'll ruin his fun.
We all know the only way he can rob a bank or jack a car is when he is armed!
If we take his gun away, he will have to break a law to cause us harm.
The IRS can help us make sure that he has done a background check twice
Once when he turns it in, then again with his 1099 on the income from his heists.

Commercial Break—This ad shows a mindless video game about killing.
It will make a black ops-ninja-seal out of any pencil necked geek who's willing.
Then there is the new action thriller movie coming straight at you in 3D
Car chases, bomb blasts, blood and guts in glorious techni-color—rated PG.
Lastly the ad about the new energy drink that all sales records it smashes.
"Guzzle Down-Upper" will keep you going long after your system crashes.

Now back to the nightly news—(marathon programming)

The talking head has now been joined by a washed-up has-been entertainer
You know, the one that is kept by the network for causes on a retainer
We want to believe that someone knows the future, maybe like a palmist.
The end of time will happen in our life time say some Mayan alarmists.
Even though the Bible we all have access to, says clearly that no one knows
However you can't make a buck if no one is scared and that really blows
The end of time is spooky stuff and keeps the money flowing
Everything from zombie toothpaste to wigs with green hair flowing.
Even though pushing the apocalypse can make you a buck or two
It is accidents and illness lawsuits that bring in the buckaroos
We believe we are all victims of everything; no one has any responsibility,
When you are hurt in an accident, abused or are just afraid of the possibility
Lawyers like Dewy, Stickem and Howe will get money for that awful pain.
The people responsible will pay through the nose and never do that again . . . .

ENOUGH!

I stood up and turned off the TV. This country is going to hell in a hand basket!

Humor is fine but the truth needs to be faced before they close the casket.

God gave us the power to pray, praise, reason and decide how to behave

Until we take that responsibility our silly butts He won't even try to save.

Alcohol doesn't kill people, drunks who think they aren't responsible do.

As long as they make the decision to drink the stuff they will be fools.

Guns don't kill people, mindless idiots who want power over others do.

As long as they are shown joys of killing by movies and games they will be fools

Silly laws don't just appear on the books, ignorant, corrupt legislators make them.

If they continue to sell themselves like prostitutes, eventually hell will bake them.

Homosexuality is not the issue but another symptom of wrongheaded thinking.

As long as people turn away from God not giving him the praise he is seeking.

Goofs wanting to act out and marry each other is the least of our worries.

That is just a red herring the devil is using along with a lot of other flurries.

We just have to have patience with them and adhere to Jesus' command

Just love them like any other; don't judge what they do, don't try to reprimand.

Let's let the insurance companies work out how they divvy their proceeds.

For me it's clear that the Bible says what sexes and pairs a marriage needs.

We don't need to stand on the street with signs berating those clowns.

Let's just let them deal with God to try and convince Him they're on solid grounds.

Lawyers don't cause lawsuits, morons who want something for nothing do.

As long as they feel that they are owed a living they will be fools too.

Waste products don't pollute, greedy morons with no regard for others do

As long as there is money in it, those knuckle draggers will be fools too.

I have thought long and hard about this and it seems appropriate to say

I feel like our America is on the way down like the Titanic; a ship of fools today.

It is apparent that it's us who should shoulder all the blame.

To say the cause is anything else is just playing the devil's game.

The bottom line of the poem has come at long, long last.

The time for ending it gracefully has long since past.

I will end it with one of the dire predictions from the Bible for the end times

It is so important it must be understood; I will print it as it is, forgoing the rhymes.

Romans 1:20 thru 1:32—Holy Bible, New International Version (with some editorial comments)

For since the creation of the world God's invisible qualities—his eternal power and divine nature—have been clearly seen, being understood from what has been made so that men are without excuse.

For although they knew God, they neither glorified him as God nor gave thanks to him, but their thinking became futile and their foolish hearts were darkened. Although they claimed to be wise, they became fools and exchanged the glory of the immortal God for images made to look like mortal man and birds and animals and reptiles.

Therefore God gave them over *(He gave up on them because they gave up on Him)* in the sinful desires of their hearts to sexual impurity and the degrading of their bodies with one another. *(Marriage is so old fashioned, don't you think?)* They exchanged the truth of God for a lie, and worshiped and served created things *(how about that Mother Nature)* rather than the Creator—who is forever praised, amen.

Because of this, God gave them over *(let them have their own way)* to shameful lusts. Even their women exchanged natural relations for unnatural ones *(became lesbians)* In the same way the men abandoned natural relations with women and were inflamed with lust for one another *(Homosexuality, the alternative life style).* Men committed indecent acts with other men *(sodomy and oral sex)* and received the due penalty for their perversion. *(No commitment, no trust, rampant sexually transmitted diseases)* Furthermore, since they did not think it worthwhile to retain the knowledge of God, he gave them over *(let them have it their way)* to a depraved mind, to do what ought not to be done. *(Abortion because the birth is so inconvenient)* They have become filled with every kind of wickedness, evil, greed and depravity. They are full of envy, murder, strife, deceit, and malice. They are gossips, slanderers, God-haters, insolent arrogant and boastful; they invent ways of doing evil; they disobey their parents; they are senseless, faithless, heartless, ruthless. *(Sound like anybody you know?)* Although they know God's righteous decree that those who do such things deserve death, they not only continue to do those very things but also approve of those who practice them.

I cannot top this quote so this poem I gladly end.
Don't worry; it won't be put on an e-mail chain letter to send.

Where Does the Darkness Go?

By William Lynn Smith

Where does the darkness go when we turn on the light?
Does it run into the closet, hiding there in fright?
Does it slide across the floor melting into the grates,
watching from its hiding place because of the light it hates?
The light doesn't hate the darkness, nor does it have any fears
It just shows up and no matter how faint, darkness disappears.
If that is so and it doesn't leave, that means it is still around.
The light can transform the darkness from the sky down to the ground.
Surroundings are the same only now not hidden behind a screen.
The darkness has turned into light and all things can be seen.
The light may sometimes show us things that we do not want to see.
But it cannot hurt us like the darkness, when we bang our knee.

It is the same with our lives as we travel along our way.
When we are children our world is full of the light of day.
But as we grow up and the worlds "wisdom" begins to matter
Our childhood's light starts to dim and the darkness begins to gather.
The darkness causes us to stumble, making us slow and afraid.
It hides the hazards of the path we travel on and we lose our way.
Despondency, anger and frustration hide like thugs ready to pounce.
Like robbers they fall on us and drain us slowly by the ounce.
They use stress like a dagger, plunging it into our side,
fear is magnified by the darkness and we are weakened by our pride.
Finally we come to the edge of some fearsome precipice,
we know that we must stop but we are sliding on the ice.
Everything we have tried has failed, vanished in the air;
Now we know what we should have done first, was turn to God in prayer!

The eloquence of speech in your prayer is not important to God,

after all, He is the creator of all things, so He won't think it odd.

Just pour out your heart, empty it of the darkness and the fright

God's presence will take that darkness and turn it into light.

We may still be standing beside a cliff high and fearsome

But as He said "I will be with you in trouble" and then some.

The problem is still there and just as dangerous, that's true.

But now it will be easy to avoid it, with God's light around you.

So what do we want around us as we travel through our life?

Do we want the darkness, that generates hatred and strife?

I believe I would rather have the light of Jesus in my heart.

To be a "light unto my path" dispelling the all of the dark.

Not only will it light the road ahead as I go along my way

But it will let others around me clearly see the light of day.

So we now know where the darkness goes when the light comes to be.

It receives the salvation of God that transforms it into the light you see.

Why William Lynn Smith

I have always been afraid to ask God why.
When people get hurt and old dogs die.
I have heard it said all my life; God is in Control
But way down deep inside, that always left me cold.
I really don't understand why a mother loses a child
It is a mystery why people are hurt when a man goes wild.
Why is it that a marriage just seems to slowly crumble?
Why a person high in esteem takes a messy tumble.

If God is in control, is He so vengeful, so narrow in his expectations;
That he strikes us down because we are not perfect in our relations.
Would it have been different if the dead child's mother had been faithful?
Would the faithful in the crowd have been hurt by the mad man hateful?
I know my Nancy was faithful. She loved her Jesus and never asked why.
So way down deep inside I really don't understand why God allowed her to die.
What did she do wrong?
Why wasn't her life long?
Why was that vile disease allowed to desecrate her? That seems so lame.
If God wanted her in His Heaven, why didn't just walk with her without the pain?

I know the printed answer that the Bible has in its pages.
Some even say that it is for our sins that we collect our wages.
I know that for this reason we are called the faithful, that's good for me
Because Jesus painfully died on the cross to show the way we must be.
I will never understand why the love of my life died in such a way.
But I do understand that I am not God, no not even for one day.
His thoughts are higher than my thoughts; His ways are higher than mine
So I really don't have the ability to understand even if he took the time.
My job is to simply carry on, to take one day and then another
To care for my family, my new wife, my sister, brother and mother.
'Til at last it is my turn at the gate, I will pray really fervent,
That when I meet Jesus he will say "Well done, My good and faithful servant."

William 1.0 by William Lynn Smith

I look at myself and wonder;

Why I'm beginning to hurt and ache.

I think about my latest blunder.

Thank Goodness no glass did break.

Sometimes it doesn't take much to agitate.

I'm sure it is because my patience is lacking.

Loss of my physicality certainly does frustrate;

It is probably life's loads that I've been packing.

Or is it the age that I find myself now?

My hand's grip seems to be lessening some.

To say that arthritis is on me, I won't allow.

To profess that over me is really dumb.

Nope, I am William 1.0, a very unique man.

To a pity party you're not invited, even in a Rolls Royce

Because you see my life is part of God's plan.

You can love me or not so much, that is your choice

That is all it is, I'm just me but that's OK;

If you don't care for me, I'll miss you; just go away.

Words by William Lynn Smith

Did you ever wish you hadn't said what you said?
You know, like "I hate you" or "I wish he was dead"
How once the words were out you couldn't take them back
Now they hang around your neck like a nasty old sack
No matter how you try, once the words are spoken
You can't repair a friend's heart that you have carelessly broken.
"Oh, you know how I am. When I get angry my blood starts to boil".
Lame excuses are spewed profusely out like used motor oil
Really they are more useless words that always make matters worse,
Now you wish that been more considerate and thoughtful first.
Finally, like a trapped animal you give up in capitulation
And try to say "I'm sorry" or something like that in frustration

There is no "reset" button. No "do over" key in real life
The Bible says that we should think before releasing strife.
That thing Jesus told us to do, you know, love one another
Instead of gossiping about him try helping your brother.
The answer to our problem is less mouth and more hand.
Less useless words and more constructive actions will heal our land.

So here is the secret to a long and happy life on earth
More important than your looks or even your girth.
Always taste each word before releasing it.
Practice holding back on answering a bit.
When conversing, thoughtful silence is a wonderful tool.
It slows down comments made that can make you look like a fool.
So when you feel the need to make a statement about yourself
Let your actions do your talking for you. Put your ego on the shelf.

Behold the T.W.I.T. by William Lynn Smith

Behold the T.W.I.T.: **T**otally **W**ithout **I**ntelligent **T**hought
Smoothest person on the planet; until they're caught
They all are unique individuals and I don't want to be unkind,
But to a person, they believe the rest of us are deaf dumb and blind.
One of the first symptoms of a new TWIT is an unerring sense,
Of being able to just skirt the truth while staying on the fence.
When they experience success in that somewhat dubious behavior,
The result is usually a short lived victory; not very long to savor.
For being caught in a lie without escape, is the bane of all TWITS
Their escape route is any story, no matter how ridiculous, that fits.
Rather than cause a ruckus or start some sort of altercation.
It is best to just let the "talking dog lie" to reduce your frustration.

Another symptom of TWIT is overuse of the response "I know"
Usually followed closely by the statement "here, let me show . . ."
It doesn't matter how much expertise they have on the issue.
Their bumbling and fumbling will bring tears requiring a tissue.
Their whole idea is to convince you that they are smarter by far,
They'll demonstrate this by lowering themselves to where you are.
It really doesn't matter how badly they screw up showing you how;
Just keep them from hurting themselves or anyone else now.
The best way to handle this situation with grace
Is to allow the TWIT some latitude to save face.

The worst kind of TWIT is the one that is behind a steering wheel.
I have no scientific data to back this up; it is just the way I feel.
The TWITS sometimes take the guise of Safety Sam, that old scamp!
Stopping on the thru-way to let someone creep out of the on ramp.
Old Sam rarely suffers the consequences of his stopping decision.
However several cars back someone usually has a rear on collision.
Then there is good ol' Timid Tammy who really should be afraid
If she knew what folks are thinking while following in her parade.

No list of twits would be complete without that Racecar Rick

He thinks he can zip though traffic 'cause he knows every trick.

Passing on the shoulder; cutting people off; while reading his tablet page,

Usually old Rick is in the news; the target of someone's road rage.

Then there is the social media butterfly that must stay in touch.

They are on the roadway; the right speed in a lane? Not so much.

You know the kind, like a drunk they will wander all over the lane;

While drinking coffee; texting their friends; being a real pain.

How many tweets can a TWIT text if a TWIT could tweet a text.

How do we react to these folks? Do we worry about what is next?

Nah! Life is too short to lose any sleep over these clowns;

Just don't get in their way; it's better to find another way around.

Keep your humor but don't make too much fun of them

Just remember at any given time you may be one of them!